SADDLE
Up!

239

Riding and Competitions
for
HORSE LOVERS

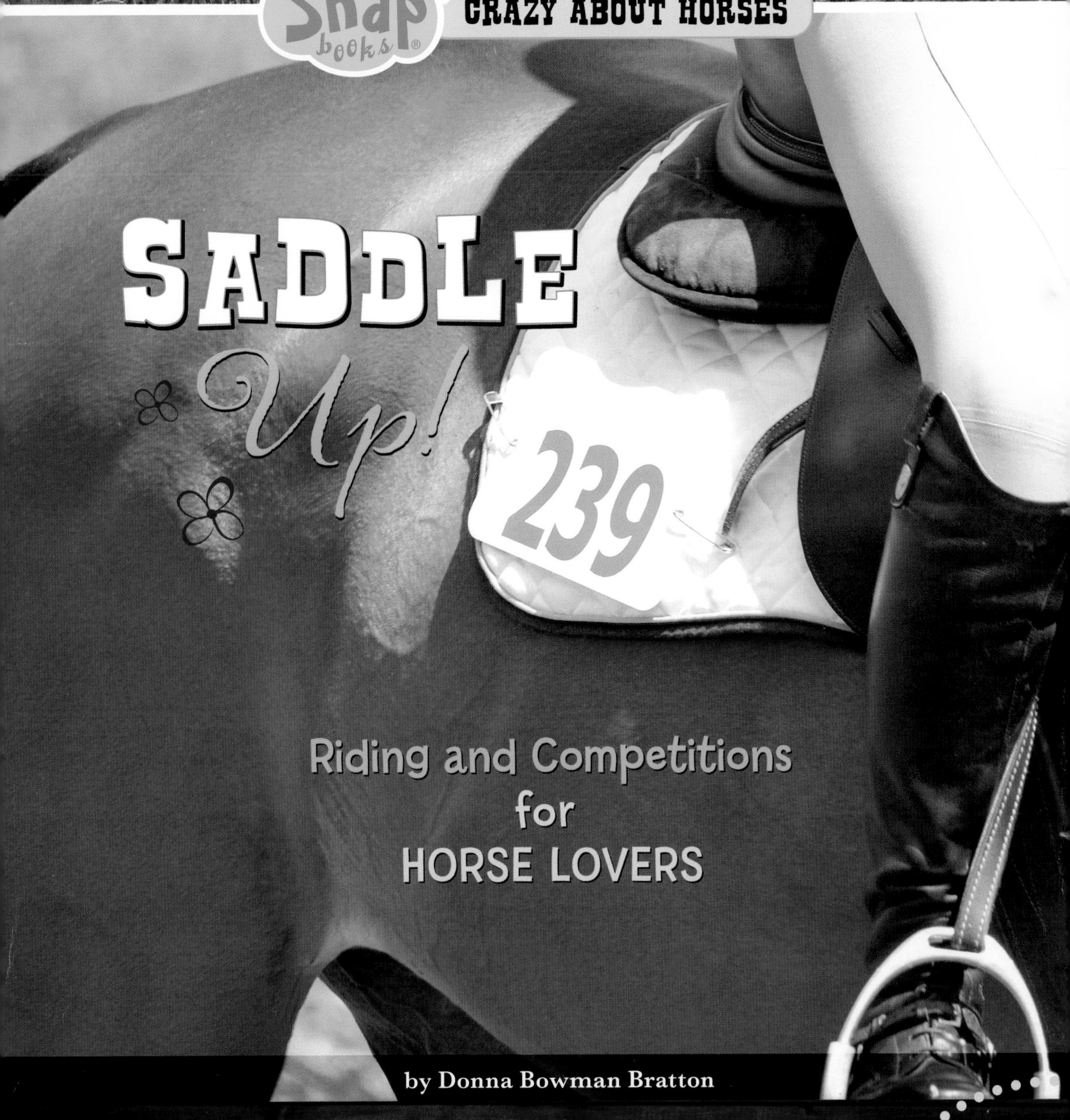

by Donna Bowman Bratton

Consultant:
Clay A. Cavinder, PhD, PAS
Associate Professor
Animal Science Department
Texas A&M University

CAPSTONE PRESS
a capstone imprint

Snap Books are published by Capstone Press,
1710 Roe Crest Drive, North Mankato, Minnesota 56003
www.capstonepub.com

Library of Congress Cataloging-in-Publication Data
Bratton, Donna Bowman, author.
Saddle up! : riding and competitions for horse lovers / by
Donna Bowman Bratton.
pages cm. — (Snap books. Crazy about horses)
Summary: "Photos and text introduce readers to riding
competitions and training, including different riding styles,
various competitions, and clothing and equipment needed for
both horse and rider"— Provided by publisher.
Audience: Ages 8–14.
Audience: Grades 4 to 6.
Includes bibliographical references and index.
ISBN 978-1-4914-0711-0 (library binding)
ISBN 978-1-4914-0717-2 (eBook PDF)
1. Horsemanship—Juvenile literature. 2. Horse shows—Juvenile
literature. 3. Horses—Training—Juvenile literature. I. Title.
SF309.2.B73 2015
798.2—dc23   2014008090

Editorial Credits
Michelle Hasselius, editor; Juliette Peters and Kazuko Collins,
designers; Deirdre Barton, media researcher; Laura Manthe,
production specialist

Photo Credits
Capstone Studio: Karon Dubke, 8, 9, 14; CLiX Photography:
Shawn Hamilton, 13 (top), 16, 21 (all), 25 (t); Corbis: Bettmann,
27; Getty Images Inc: Boston Globe, 5 (t); Highland Photography
by Darcie Strobach, 17, 23, 24, 28 (b); Shutterstock: Abramova
Kseniya, cover, acceptphoto, 29 (b), Anastasila Golokova, horse
silhouette design element, andersphoto, tooled floral leather
design element, Bernd Leitner Fotodesign, 19 (b), bikeriderlondon,
6, De Visu, 11 (b), Debby Wong, 5 (b), defotoberg, 28 (t),
donatas1205, square leather pieces design element, fotoedu, 20,
Kenneth Sponsler, 11 (t), Kondrashov Mikhail Evgenevich, 22, 29
(t), mariait, 4, marikond, 15, meunierd, 1, Neale Cousland, back
cover, 26, nuttakit, brown leather strip design, Perry Correll, 2–3,
25 (b), PhotoHouse, 32, Reinhold Leitner, wood design element,
Rita Kochmarjova, 18, Robynrg, 7, Tamara Didenko, 19 (t), thinz,
stripe design, flower design elements, tjwvandongen, 31, Todd
Klassy, 10, Vanessa Nel, 12, Vera Zinkova, 13 (b)

Glossary terms are bolded on first use in text.

Printed in the United States of America in North Mankato, Minnesota.
032014   008087CGF14

TABLE of CONTENTS

RIDING *a Horse*

Does the thought of riding a horse make you think of freedom, speed, or grace? You're not alone. Horses have shaped history for thousands of years. Before the invention of the automobile and railroads, people depended on horses for all sorts of things. Soldiers relied on horses in war times. The postal service delivered mail on horseback. Farmers used horses to plow fields and haul heavy loads. Horse-drawn **carriages** and wagons did the work of today's cars, trucks, ambulances, taxis, and more. Today most American horses are considered family pets, ranch horses, or show partners.

JUST WHAT THE DOCTOR ORDERED

Scientists have proven what horse lovers have known for some time—being around horses makes people happy. It's no wonder horses make great therapy animals. Hospital patients can benefit from a friendly visit from a specially trained miniature horse. Some minis are even trained as guide animals for people with vision problems.

Doctors and physical therapists can include horses in therapy treatments for people with injuries, disabilities, or emotional problems. This is called **hippotherapy**. Hippotherapy uses the rhythm and repetition of horse riding to increase a patient's muscle strength, balance, and flexibility.

DID YOU KNOW?

Celebrities love horses too. Taylor Swift, Hilary Duff, Britney Spears, Johnny Depp, and Kaley Cuoco are all horse riders.

Taylor Swift

TWO-LEGGED and FOUR-LEGGED *Athletes*

Horse riding is a sport, and a horse and rider are athletes. Riders need good **posture**, balance, and strength in the saddle. Riding a horse is great exercise. People interested in riding should stay active or get involved in team sports. Regular exercise builds strength needed to be a good rider.

It's best to choose a riding style and competition that fits both horse and rider. Are you good at some activities but not so good at others? Horses are the same way. A shorter horse may not be cut out for jumping. A horse that isn't flexible won't do well in dressage. A horse that gets scared easily probably won't make a good competitive trail horse. A horse with a slow, laid-back personality is probably not right for speed events like barrel racing. If you plan to compete, remember that it takes practice, patience, and time to become a winning team.

polo

SAFE RIDING TIPS

Here are some tips to remember before riding a horse.
- Always ride with adult supervision.
- Horse and rider should warm up before riding.
- Always wear a safety helmet and boots.
- Only use riding equipment that is in good, clean condition.
- Horses should be groomed before and after riding.
- Watch for holes or obstacles on the ground that could cause a horse to stumble.
- Never ride in the dark.
- Don't startle a horse from behind—they may kick.

DID YOU KNOW?

It's important to start a new exercise routine slowly to avoid injury.

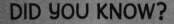

Riding TACK

The equipment used for horseback riding is called tack. Basic tack includes a saddle and a **bridle**. Western and English saddles sit right behind the horse's shoulder blades, on saddle pads. The saddles are designed to spread the rider's weight evenly across the horse's back. They are secured with a girth, which is a strap that stretches under the narrowest part of a horse's belly. Just like people, each horse has a different body shape. It's important to choose a saddle that fits a horse's shape.

It's also important to choose a bridle that fits. A bridle is like a horse's headgear. It holds a metal **bit** in the horse's mouth. The rider uses reins attached to the bit to guide the horse.

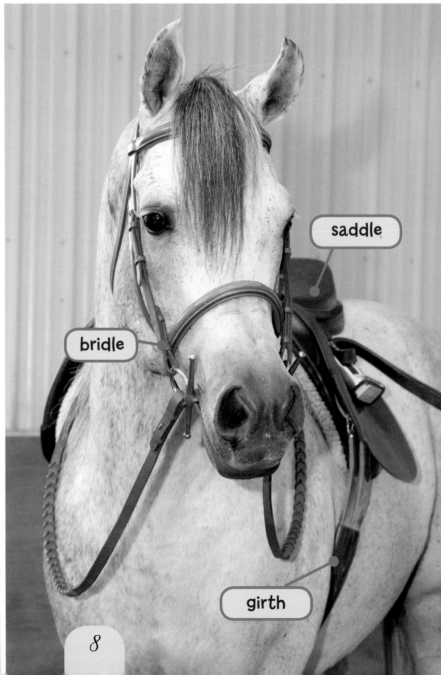

saddle

bridle

girth

SLOW TO SPEEDY: RIDING GAITS

The speed of a horse is called a **gait**. There are different gaits for English and Western riding.

ENGLISH

walk—a relaxed pace

trot—faster than the Western jog; it's too bumpy for a rider to sit comfortably. Instead the rider rises out of the saddle in rhythm with the horse.

canter—the English version of the Western lope

gallop—the horse takes longer steps than in a lope or canter but moves slower than when it's running

WESTERN

walk—a relaxed pace

jog—the horse takes longer steps to cover more ground; the rider still sits comfortably in the saddle

lope—faster than a trot but slower than a gallop

gallop—the horse takes longer steps than in a lope or canter but moves slower than when it's running

trot

WESTERN
Riding Competitions

A rider who daydreams about ranch life as an American cowgirl or cowboy might enjoy Western riding. These ranchers take care of wounded animals, move herds of cattle, repair fences, and check food and water in all types of weather. Western riders need a calm, comfortable, quick horse. Today there are riding competitions that test the kind of horse-rider teamwork needed on a ranch.

COWGIRL COMFORT

Ranchers can spend days or even weeks in the saddle, tending to livestock. The deep seat and long stirrups of a Western saddle are comfortable for long rides.

Today's Western saddles are specialized for different riding events. Show saddles and bridles often have fancy silver trimmings. For most Western horse show events, riders wear long-sleeved shirts, jeans, boots, and Western hats. **Chaps** are also stylish.

DID YOU KNOW?

A rider traditionally **mounts** a horse from the left side. This dates back to a time when ancient soldiers first rode horses into battle. Right-handed warriors carried their swords on their left hips. Mounting from the left kept riders from injuring their horses— or stabbing themselves in the foot!

CUTTING
Competitions

Sometimes ranchers need to separate, or cut, a cow from a large herd. This is done to give the cow medicine or treat an injury. This basic ranch duty led to cutting competitions. It takes an advanced rider with a horse that's trained around cows to compete.

In cutting competitions a small herd of cattle is gathered at one end of an arena. Competitors ride quietly into the herd and push one cow away. Like a soccer goalie watching the opposing team, a cutting horse is trained to predict a cow's movements. When the cow tries to run back to the herd, the horse crouches low and moves quickly. If the cow moves too fast, the horse spins around and runs to block it. Horse and rider must keep the cow away from the herd for 2.5 minutes.

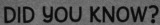

DID YOU KNOW?
Most Western riders hold the reins in one hand. On a ranch the free hand can hold a lasso or other tools.

The quarter horse is the most popular breed for Western riding events like cutting.

Barrel RACING

DID YOU KNOW?

The fastest barrel racers have completed the cloverleaf pattern in less than 13.5 seconds.

Barrel racing began in Texas and gave women a rodeo sport all their own. Today men are barrel racers too, but girls still rule the sport.

This might be the right sport for a rider who likes speed. Barrel racers enter the competition arena at a full run. They aim for three large barrels arranged in a triangle. The goal is to race in a cloverleaf pattern around the barrels without knocking one over. It takes practice to make tight turns around each barrel and then regain full speed in about two steps. If a barrel is knocked over, there is a time penalty. At the end of the event, the rider with the fastest time wins.

DID YOU KNOW?

Horses that compete in barrel racing, cutting, jumping, and other active events wear protective leg wraps or boots.

Trail RIDING

For riders who like obstacle courses, trail competitions might be a perfect fit. Riders are judged on their ability to **maneuver** their horses through patterns of difficult challenges. Horses are judged on agility, willingness, and calmness.

The pattern isn't announced until the morning of the event, so riders have to memorize it quickly. Horse and rider must work as a team. Patterns might call for competitors to jog over logs, cross a wooden bridge, or slosh through water. A trail horse can't get scared if a rider is asked to pick up a noisy tarp, rattle a can of pebbles, or pull a strange object out of a mailbox. Points are deducted if the pattern is not completed or if obstacles are knocked over.

ENGLISH
Riding Competitions

English riding may be a great choice for people who want to ride horses like British royalty. This riding style began long ago in the European military. It later became the preferred style for English fox hunting and racing sports. It is still a formal style of riding. Today there are many English riding competitions to choose from.

PETITE SEAT

The small English saddles were designed to allow horses better movement at different speeds and over jumps. They come in different styles for events like dressage, jumping, and polo. Riders using English saddles have closer leg contact with their horses. The shorter stirrups allow the rider to rise out of the saddle in rhythm with the horse's trot. This up and down motion is called posting.

For competitions a rider wears a show jacket called a hunt coat, as well as **breeches**, riding boots, and a helmet. Some events require gloves too. A rider's hair must be above the collar. English bridles have a simple bit.

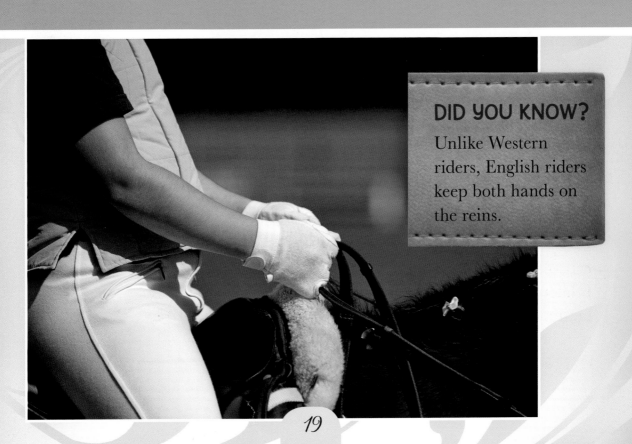

DID YOU KNOW?

Unlike Western riders, English riders keep both hands on the reins.

Show JUMPING

Show jumping is like jumping hurdles at a track meet. Horses must have long, lean bodies, good jumping **instincts**, and powerful legs. There are jumping classes for ponies too.

Riders sit in a position called forward seat. Riders keep their backs straight and bend their legs, so their hips are directly above their ankles. They must keep their weight balanced in both stirrups. If they lose their balance, riders can fall off. A rider shifts his or her weight out of the saddle, just as the horse lifts off the ground to jump. This relieves the weight from the horse's back.

Competitions take place in an arena with a pattern of colorful hurdles that look like fences. In addition to clearing the hurdles, competitors may have to jump two rails instead of one or leap over a pool of water.

Some professional show jumpers can clear hurdles that are 7 feet (2.1 meters) high.

DID YOU KNOW?

Three English riding events are part of the Olympic games—show jumping, dressage, and eventing. Eventing is like a triathlon, where riders compete in dressage, show jumping, and cross-country riding.

DRESSAGE

Riders who enjoy gymnastics or ballet may like dressage. Dressage is a French word that means training, but it should mean dancing. Horses are taught to change the length of their steps and flex their necks and bodies. Their movements look like a dance. Horses can trot and canter in one spot, spin on one foot, or extend their gaits to look like they are floating. The most experienced dressage horses can even learn fancy kicks.

PASSING THE TEST

Many people consider dressage the highest form of horse training. It can take eight or nine years for a horse and rider to pass through the nine training levels of dressage. To advance to the next training level, horse and rider must pass tests at competitions.

At dressage competitions, horse and rider teams perform alone in an arena. Lettered markers are placed around the arena to mark where certain gait changes or movements are required. Riders and their horses must perform each skill at the designated markers.

DRESSING UP FOR DRESSAGE

A dressage rider wears a long, dark riding jacket, white shirt, white tie, white or tan breeches, black boots, white gloves, and a helmet or top hat. The saddle is wider and has longer stirrups.

A horse's mane and tail are braided for dressage competitions. Tiny braids are often folded into little balls, forming **button braids**.

DID YOU KNOW?

Before beginning a performance, a dressage competitor must nod to the judge in a salute. He or she must salute before leaving the arena as well.

Horse RACING

0 9 8 7 6 5

Horse racing competitions have been around for as long as people have ridden horses. The muscular quarter horse is the fastest breed in shorter races. They can run .25 miles (.4 kilometers) in less than 21 seconds. But the long, lean body of the Thoroughbred makes it the fastest breed for long distance races. On race day horses are loaded into the starting stalls on the racetrack. The starting gate opens and the horses bolt forward, starting the clock.

The race is on!

Jockeys ride racehorses. They wear race uniforms called silks. Unlike most athletes, jockeys must be strong but small. There are strict rules about how much weight a racehorse is allowed to carry. Some races allow no more than 110 pounds (50 kilograms) total, including the saddle. Luckily racing saddles weigh little more than 1 pound (.5 kg). If the jockey and saddle don't weigh enough, weighted saddle pads are added.

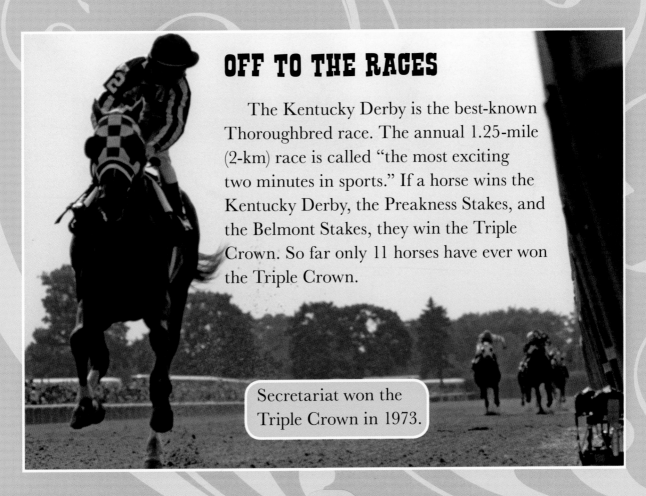

OFF TO THE RACES

The Kentucky Derby is the best-known Thoroughbred race. The annual 1.25-mile (2-km) race is called "the most exciting two minutes in sports." If a horse wins the Kentucky Derby, the Preakness Stakes, and the Belmont Stakes, they win the Triple Crown. So far only 11 horses have ever won the Triple Crown.

Secretariat won the Triple Crown in 1973.

TEST YOUR HORSE RIDING IQ

1. If you want to ride like a cowboy, which riding style would you choose?
   a. dressage
   b. English
   c. Western

2. Which event includes an obstacle course?
   a. trail
   b. dressage
   c. cutting
   d. barrel racing

3. Which speed event class was created for girls?
   a. horse racing
   b. show jumping
   c. dressage
   d. barrel racing

4. Which event takes years to master and looks like a dance?
   a. barrel racing
   b. dressage
   c. trail
   d. cutting

5. Which of the following is a safe riding tip?
   a. pack snacks
   b. never sneak up on a horse from behind
   c. ride with adult supervision
   d. B and C

GLOSSARY

bit (BIT)—the metal mouthpiece of the bridle that goes in a horse's mouth

breeches (BRICH-iz)—fitted long pants worn with tall riding boots

bridle (BRYE-duhl)—the straps that fit around a horse's head and connect to a bit to control a horse while riding

button braid (BUHT-uhn BRAYD)—a horse's mane is braided to look like small buttons; popular in dressage competitions

carriage (KAYR-ij)—a vehicle that is pulled by a horse

chaps (CHAPS)—leather coverings worn over pants to protect a rider's legs

gait (GATE)—the way an animal moves at different speeds

hippotherapy (hip-oh-THAIR-uh-pee)—a treatment that uses horseback riding to help people with disabilities

instinct (IN-stingkt)—behavior that is natural rather than learned

maneuver (muh-NOO-ver)—a planned and controlled movement that requires practiced skills

mount (MOUNT)—to get on top of a horse

posture (POSS-chur)—the position of your body when sitting in a saddle

READ MORE

Dowdy, Penny. *Dressage.* Horsing Around. New York: Crabtree Pub. Co., 2010.

Gray, Susan H. *Horse Shows.* Horses! New York: Marshall Cavendish, 2013.

Young, Rae. *Drawing Barrel Racers and Other Speedy Horses.* Drawing Horses. North Mankato, Minn.: Capstone Press, 2014.

INTERNET SITES

FactHound offers a safe, fun way to find Internet sites related to this book. All of the sites on FactHound have been researched by our staff.

Here's all you do:

Visit *www.facthound.com*

Type in this code: 9781491407110

Check out projects, games and lots more at
www.capstonekids.com

INDEX